JUMPIN' JIM's
UKULELE
Gems

T0051163

Compiled by Jim Beloff

Foreword 2
How To Use This Book 3
    Tuning
    Transposing
Chord Charts 4

THE SONGS...
Button Up Your Overcoat 10
Bye, Bye Blues 56
Dear Hearts And Gentle People 12
Heart And Soul 14
I'll See You In My Dreams 16
It Had To Be You 18
It's Been A Long, Long Time 20
I Wanna Be Loved By You 22
Life Is Just A Bowl Of Cherries 24
Lullaby Of Birdland 26
Lulu's Back In Town 28
Me And My Shadow 32
Moonlight Becomes You 30
My Little Grass Shack In Kealakekua, Hawaii 33
Scratchy Records 36
Singin' In The Rain 42
Sonny Boy 44
Sunny Side Up 47
Ukulele Lady 48
Under Paris Skies 39
When The Red, Red, Robin Comes Bob, Bob, Bobbin' Along 50
Yes Sir! That's My Baby 52
You're The Cream In My Coffee 54
UKULELE CHORD SOLOS 57
Ain't She Sweet 58
All Of Me 60
Seems Like Old Times 62
Sentimental Journey 64
'Til There Was You 67
When You Wish Upon A Star 70

EXCLUSIVELY DISTRIBUTED BY

HAL•LEONARD®
CORPORATION
7777 W. BLUEMOUND RD. P.O. BOX 13819 MILWAUKEE, WI 53213

Edited by Ronny S. Schiff
Cover and Art Direction by Elizabeth Maihock Beloff
Graphics and Music Typography by Charylu Roberts

FOREWORD

If you are like me, you are always on the lookout for songs that have been arranged for the ukulele. While most of the sheet music from the 'twenties and 'thirties included uke chords, certain songs inevitably stand out. For me, one big reason is the cleverness of the uke arrangements.

In assembling this latest collection, I pulled together well-known songs with, in most cases, interesting ukulele arrangements. Songs like "Moonlight Becomes You," "Lullaby of Birdland," and the five DeSylva, Brown and Henderson compositions feature much chordal movement and almost a jazz quality to the arrangements.

I've included six chord solos to conclude the book. When played as written, these arrangements produce both the melody and chords of the song with each strum and fingering change. Some are easier than others, but all can be very satisfying to learn and perform.

"Gems" conjure up words like brilliance, sparkle, rarity, and timeless beauty. To me, these songs are gems in the truest sense of the word. Every time I play through them, I am struck by the beauty of their melodies, the sparkle of the lyrics, and the brilliance of the chords. I'm also reminded of how great a very portable and outwardly simple 4-string instrument can make them sound.

Here's to having a lot of fun polishing these gems yourself!

—Jumpin' Jim

Also Available...

• **Jim's Dog Has Fleas**—A CD of original songs for the uke by Jim Beloff.

• **Jumpin' Jim's Ukulele Favorites**—A songbook featuring 30 great songs arranged for ukulele.

• **Jumpin' Jim's Ukulele Tips 'n' Tunes**—A step-by-step method and songbook.

HOW TO USE THIS BOOK

Tuning

The smallest and most popular size of the ukulele is the soprano. All of the songs in this book were arranged for the soprano ukulele in C tuning. Nonetheless, if you tune any sized uke as shown below, you will be able to play the chords as written.

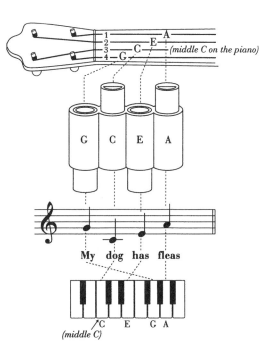

The easiest way to tune the ukulele is with a pitch pipe, matching the strings with the notes:

This corresponds to that famous melody:

Here are the notes on the keyboard:

Transposing

If any song feels too high or too low for you to sing comfortably, you may want to change its key. To do this it is necessary to change all the chords. Use this chart below that shows you the key and the related chords:

Major				Minor		
Chords in C :	C	F	G⁷	Am	Dm	E⁷
D♭:	D♭	G♭	A♭⁷	B♭m	E♭m	F⁷
D :	D	G	A⁷	Bm	Em	F♯⁷
E♭:	E♭	A♭	B♭⁷	Cm	Fm	G⁷
E :	E	A	B⁷	C♯m	F♯m	G♯⁷
F :	F	B♭	C⁷	Dm	Gm	A⁷
G♭:	G♭	C♭	D♭⁷	E♭m	A♭m	B♭⁷
G :	G	C	D⁷	Em	Am	B⁷
A♭:	A♭	D♭	E♭⁷	Fm	B♭m	C⁷
A :	A	D	E⁷	F♯m	Bm	C♯⁷
B♭:	B♭	E♭	F⁷	Gm	Cm	D⁷
B :	B	E	F♯⁷	G♯m	C♯m	D♯⁷

Strums

The songs do not indicate strums or rhythm markings. If you're looking for basic strumming suggestions, refer to *Jumpin' Jim's Ukulele Tips 'n' Tunes*.

Major Chords

1st Position

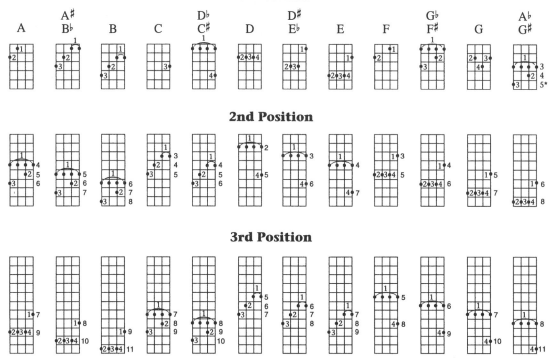

2nd Position

3rd Position

Minor Chords

1st Position

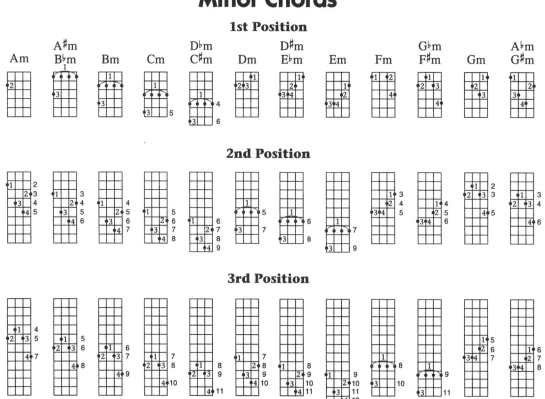

2nd Position

3rd Position

*numbers at side indicate fret

Minor Seventh Chords

1st Position

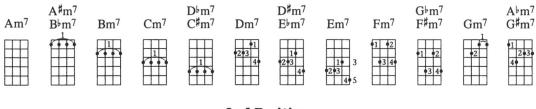

2nd Position

3rd Position

Major Sixth Chords

1st Position

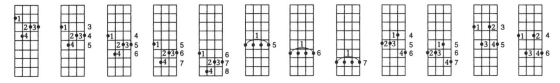

2nd Position

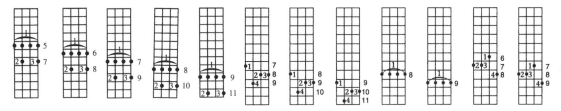

3rd Position

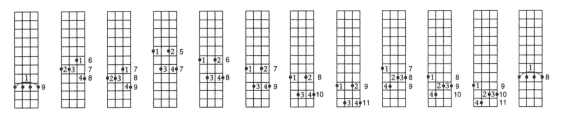

Minor Sixth Chords

1st Position

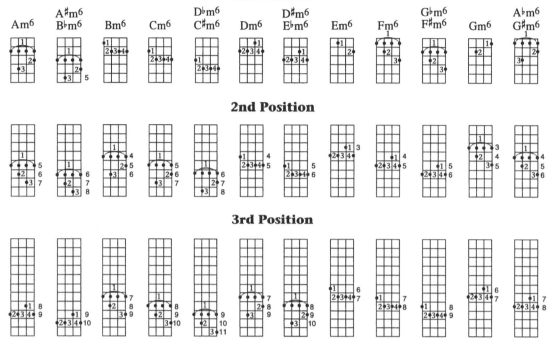

Major Seventh Chords

1st Position

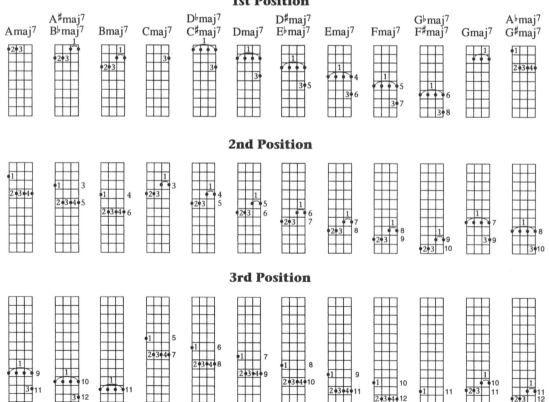

Dominant Seventh Chords

1st Position

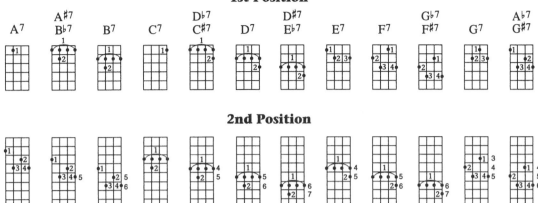

2nd Position

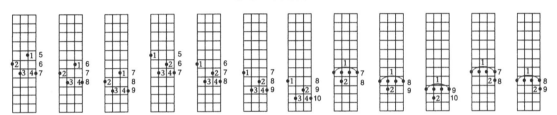

3rd Position

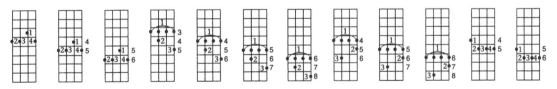

Dominant Ninth Chords

1st Position

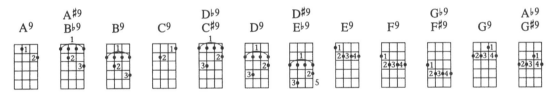

2nd Position

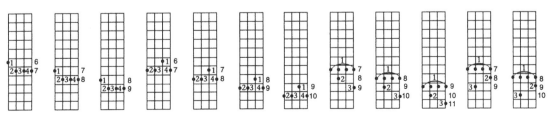

3rd Position

Dominant Seventh Chords With Raised Fifth (7th+5)

1st Position

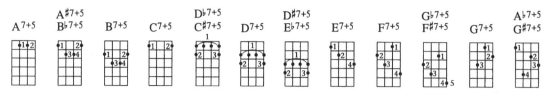

2nd Position

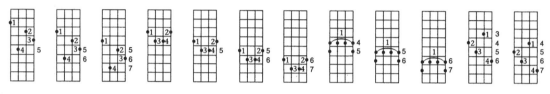

3rd Position

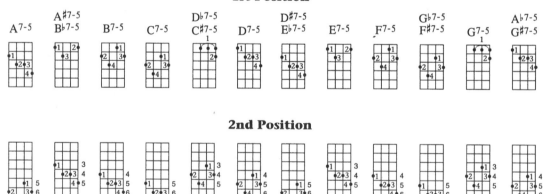

Dominant Seventh Chords With Lowered Fifth (7th-5)

1st Position

2nd Position

3rd Position

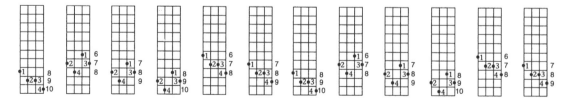

Augmented Chords

1st Position

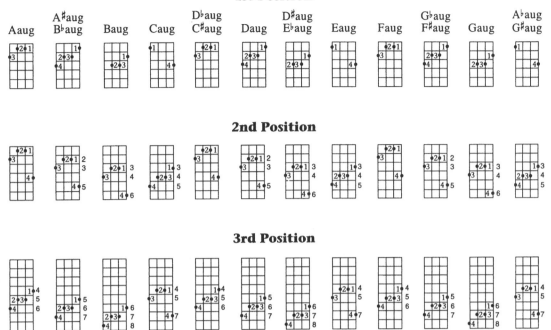

2nd Position

3rd Position

Diminished Seventh Chords

1st Position

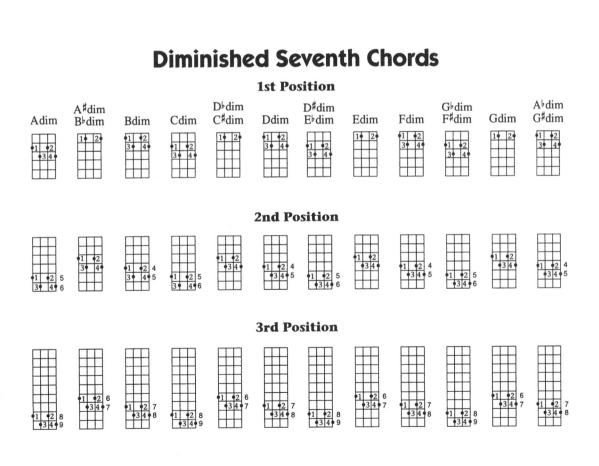

2nd Position

3rd Position

Button Up Your Overcoat

By B. G. DeSYLVA,
LEW BROWN & RAY HENDERSON

But-ton up your o - ver-coat __ when the wind is free;
But-ton up you o - ver-coat __ when the wind is free;

take good __ care of your-self, __ you be long to me! _____
take good __ care of your-self, __ you be long to me! _____

__ Eat an ap - ple ev - 'ry day, __ get to bed by
Wear your flan - nel un - der-wear, __ when you climb a

three; take good __ care of your- self, __ you be - long to me! __
tree; take good __ care of your- self, __ you be - long to me! __

Dear Hearts And Gentle People

Words by
BOB HILLIARD

Music by
SAMMY FAIN

FIRST NOTE

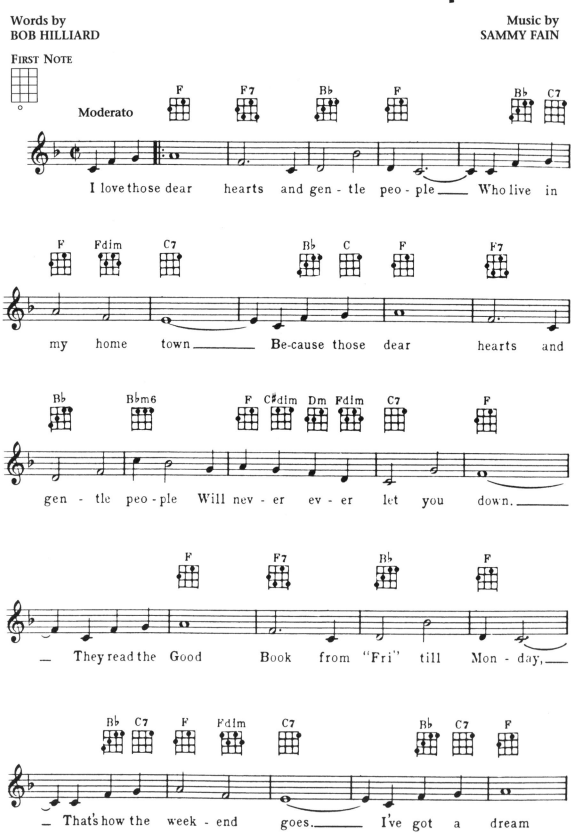

I love those dear hearts and gen-tle peo-ple___ Who live in my home town___ Be-cause those dear hearts and gen-tle peo-ple Will nev-er ev-er let you down.___ ___ They read the Good Book from "Fri" till Mon-day,___ ___ That's how the week-end goes.___ I've got a dream

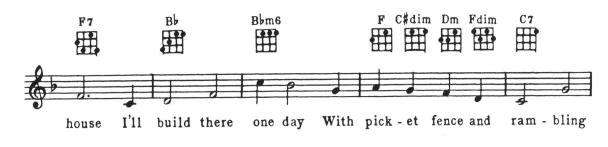

house I'll build there one day With pick-et fence and ram-bling

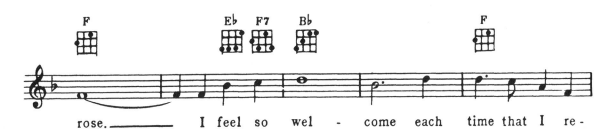

rose._____ I feel so wel - come each time that I re-

turn That my hap-py heart keeps laugh-ing like a clown.___ I love the

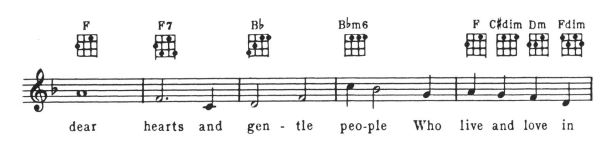

dear hearts and gen - tle peo-ple Who live and love in

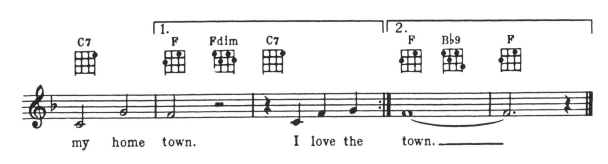

my home town. I love the town._____

Heart And Soul

Words by
FRANK LOESSER

Music by
HOAGY CARMICHAEL

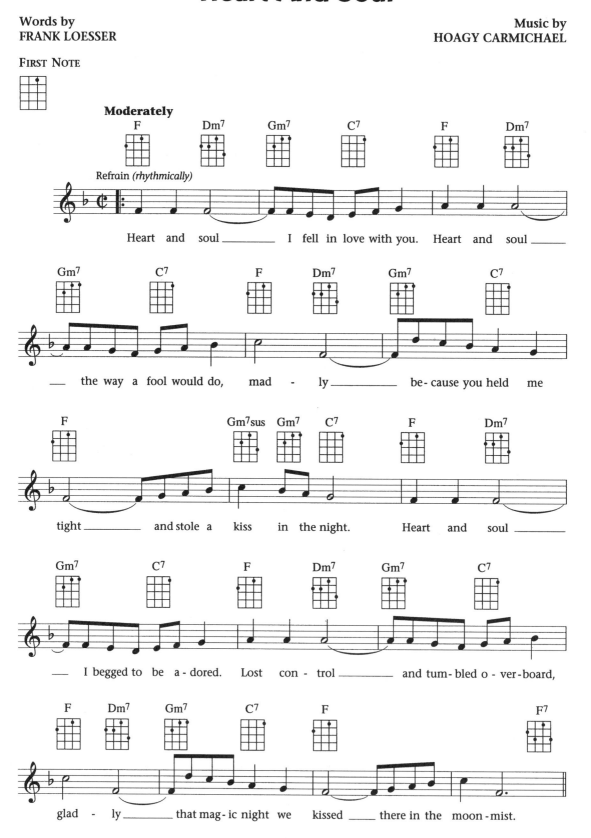

I'll See You In My Dreams

Words by
GUS KAHN

Music by
ISHAM JONES

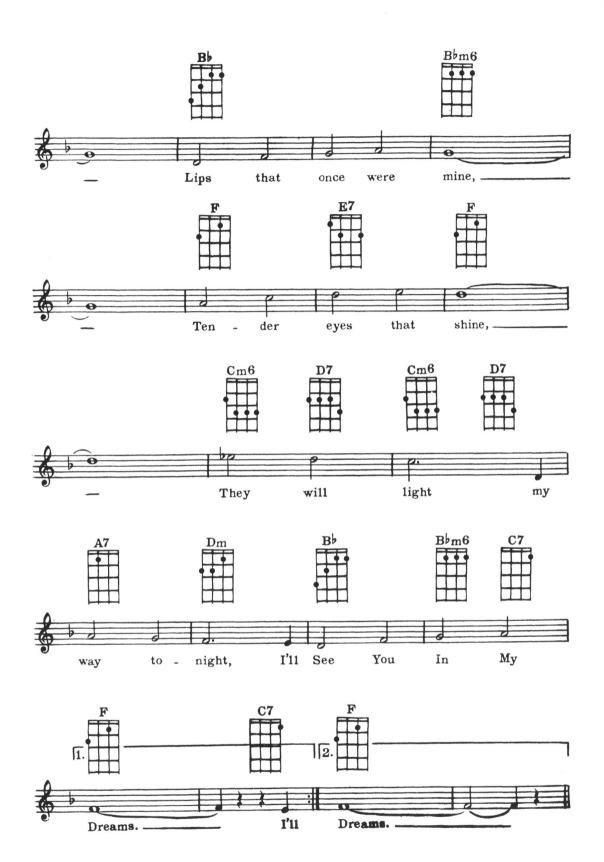

It Had To Be You

Lyrics by
GUS KAHN

Music by
ISHAM JONES

It's Been A Long, Long Time

Lyric by
SAMMY CAHN

Music by
JULE STYNE

FIRST NOTE

Just kiss me once, then kiss me twice, then kiss me once a-gain;— it's been a long, long time. Have-n't felt like this, my dear, since can't re-mem-ber when;— it's been a long, long time. You'll nev-er know how man-y dreams I dreamed a-bout you, or just how emp-ty they all seemed with-out you. So,

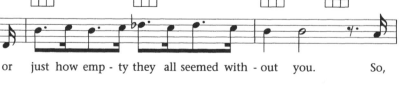

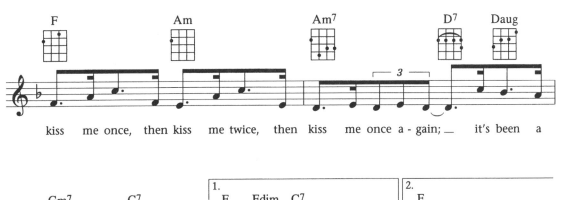

kiss me once, then kiss me twice, then kiss me once a-gain; __ it's been a

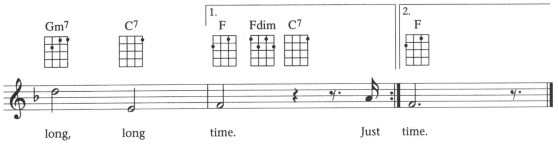

long, long time. Just time.

Flea market uke 4 sale—No reasonable offer refused!

I Wanna Be Loved By You

Words by
BERT KALMAR

Music by
HERBERT STOTHART
and HARRY RUBY

First Note

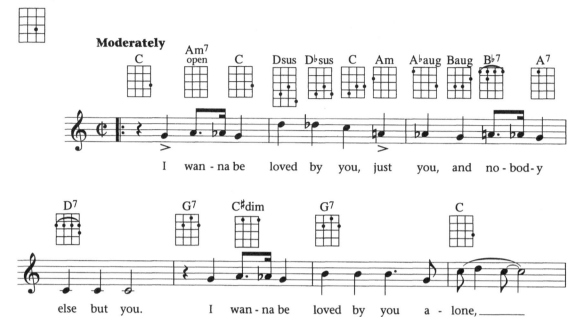

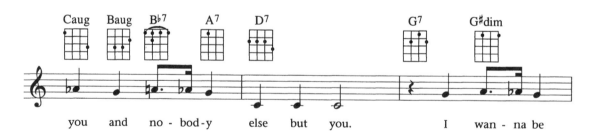

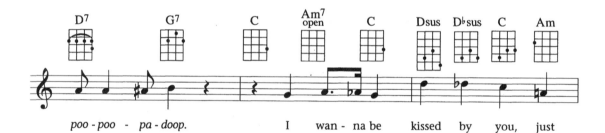

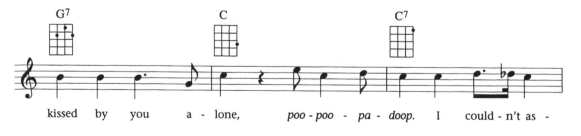

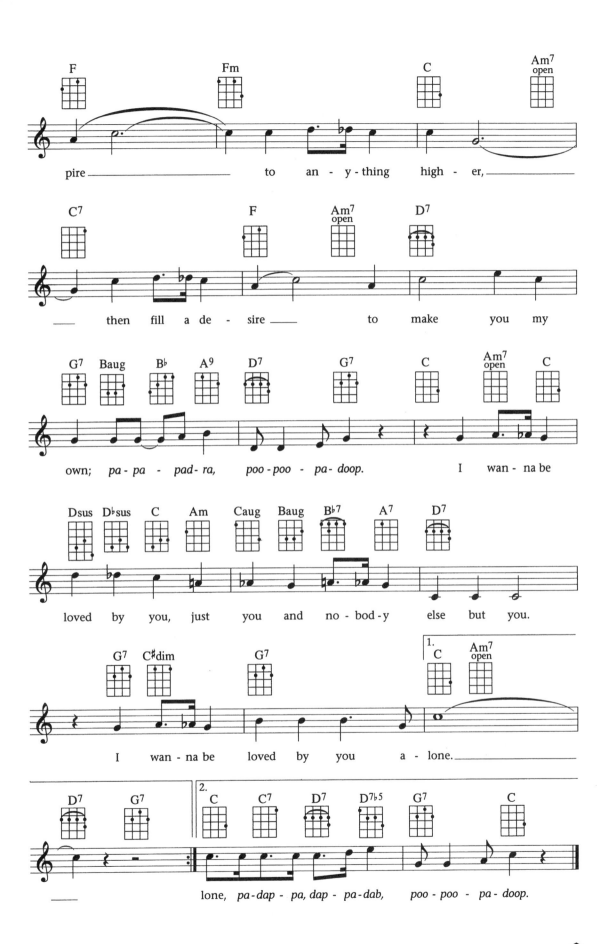

Life Is Just A Bowl Of Cherries

By LEW BROWN
and RAY HENDERSON

Life is just a bowl of cher-ries, _____ don't make it se - ri - ous, _____ life's too mys - te - ri - ous. _____ You work, you save, you wor - ry so, but you can't take your dough when you go, go, go. So keep re - peat - ing it's the ber - ries, the strong - est oak must fall. _____ The sweet things in life, — to

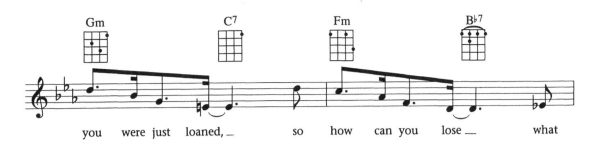

you were just loaned, — so how can you lose — what

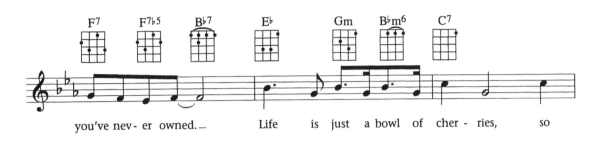

you've nev-er owned. — Life is just a bowl of cher-ries, so

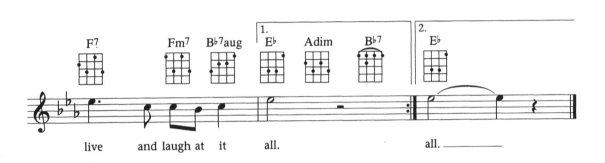

live and laugh at it all. all. _____

Henderson, Brown and DeSylva, music and lyrics for
"Button Up Your Overcoat," "Life Is Just A Bowl Of Cherries,"
"Sonny Boy," "Sunny Side Up" and "You're The Cream In My Coffee."
(Photo courtesy of Howard Henderson)

Lullaby Of Birdland

Lyric by
George David Weiss

Music by
GEORGE SHEARING

FIRST NOTE

Snappily

Lul - la - by of Bird - land that's what I — al - ways hear — when you sigh. __ Nev - er in my word - land could there be ways __ to re - veal, __ _____ in a phrase, __ how I feel! __ Have you ev - er heard two tur - tle doves — bill and coo — when they love? __ That's the kind of mag - ic mu - sic we make — with our lips _____ when we kiss! __

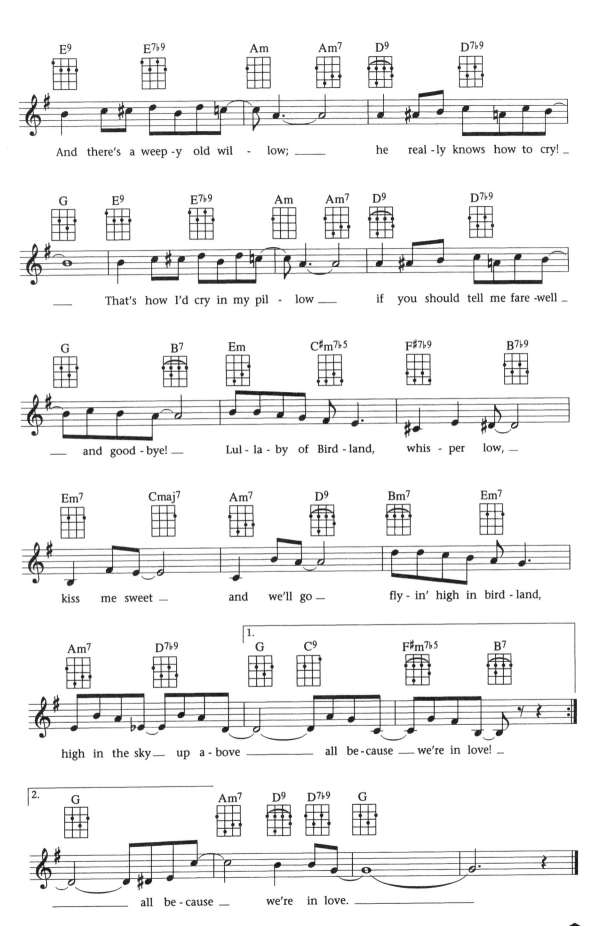

Lulu's Back In Town

Lyric by
AL DUBIN

Music by
HARRY WARREN

FIRST NOTE

Con Spirito

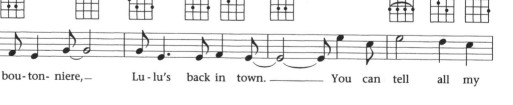

Got-ta get my old tux-e-do pressed, — got-ta sew a but-ton on my vest; — 'cause to-night I've got-ta look my best, — Lu-lu's back in town. —

———— Got-ta get a half-a-buck some-where, —

got-ta shine my shoes and slick my hair; — got-ta get my-self a bou-ton-niere, — Lu-lu's back in town. ———— You can tell all my

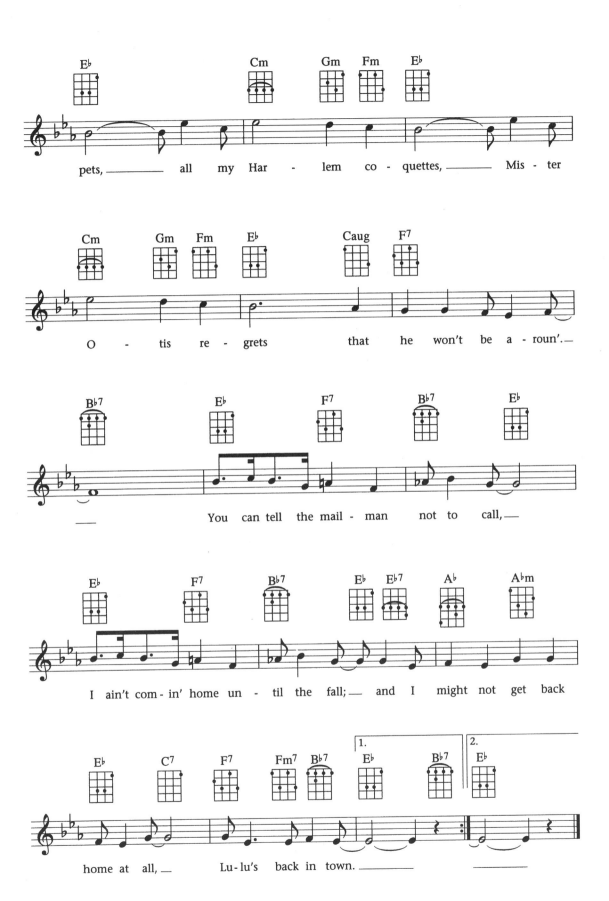

pets, _____ all my Har - lem co - quettes, _____ Mis - ter

O - tis re - grets that he won't be a - roun'. ___

___ You can tell the mail - man not to call, ___

I ain't com - in' home un - til the fall; ___ and I might not get back

home at all, ___ Lu - lu's back in town. _____ _____

Moonlight Becomes You

Words by
JOHNNY BURKE

Music by
JIMMY VAN HEUSEN

FIRST NOTE

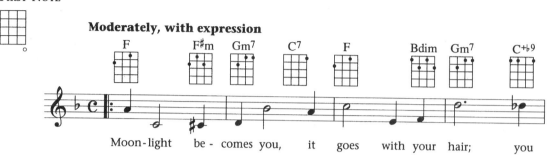

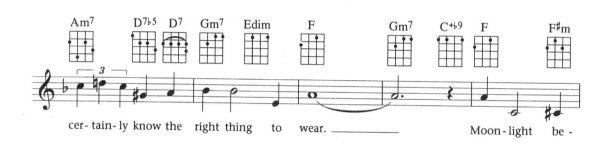

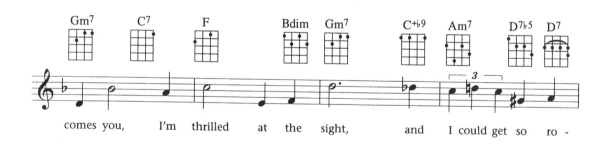

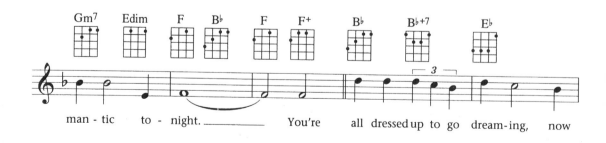

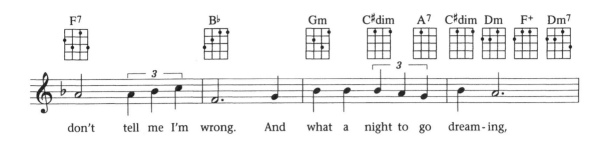

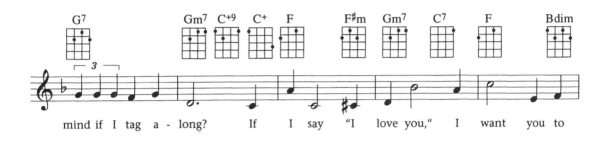

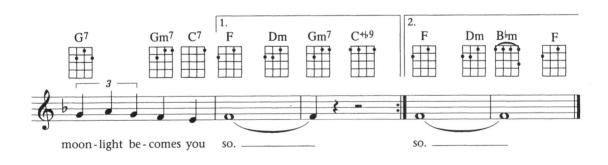

Me And My Shadow

Lyric by
BILLY ROSE

Music by
AL JOLSON and
DAVE DREYER

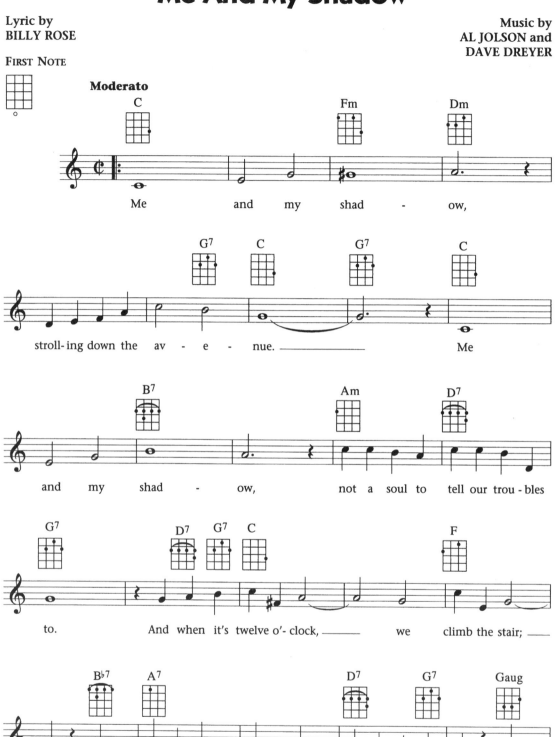

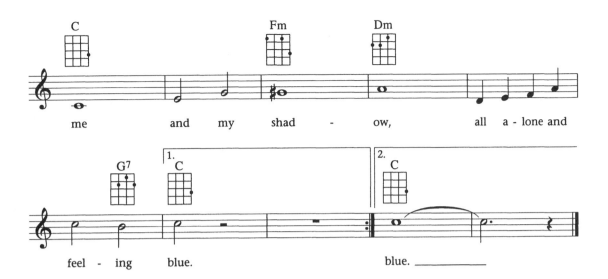

me and my shad - ow, all a - lone and feel - ing blue. blue. _____

My Little Grass Shack In
Kealakekua, Hawaii

Words and Music by
BILL COGSWELL, TOMMY HARRISON
and JOHNNY NOBLE

FIRST NOTE

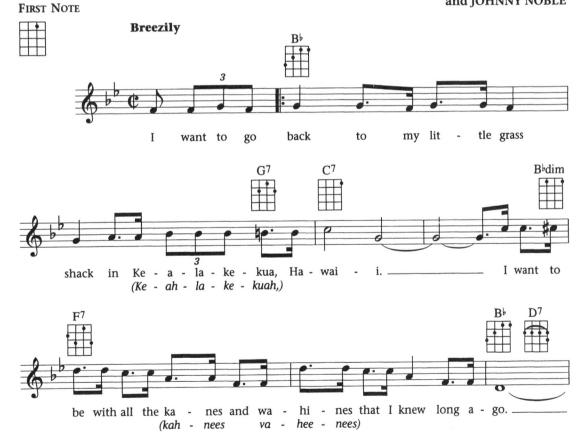

I want to go back to my lit - tle grass shack in Ke - a - la - ke - kua, Ha - wai - i. _____ I want to
(Ke - ah - la - ke - kuah,)

be with all the ka - nes and wa - hi - nes that I knew long a - go. _____
(kah - nees va - hee - nees)

I can hear old gui-tars a-play-ing on the

beach at Ho-o-nau-nau. I can hear the Ha-wai-ians
(Ho - oh - now - now)

say-ing, "Ko-mo-mai no ka-u-a i-ka
("Ko - mo - myee kah-oo - ah e - cah

ha-le we-la-ka-hao." It won't be long 'til my ship will be sail-ing back to
hah - lee vay - la - ka - how")

Ko-na; a grand old place that's al-ways fair to

see. I'm just a lit-tle Ha-wai-ian and a

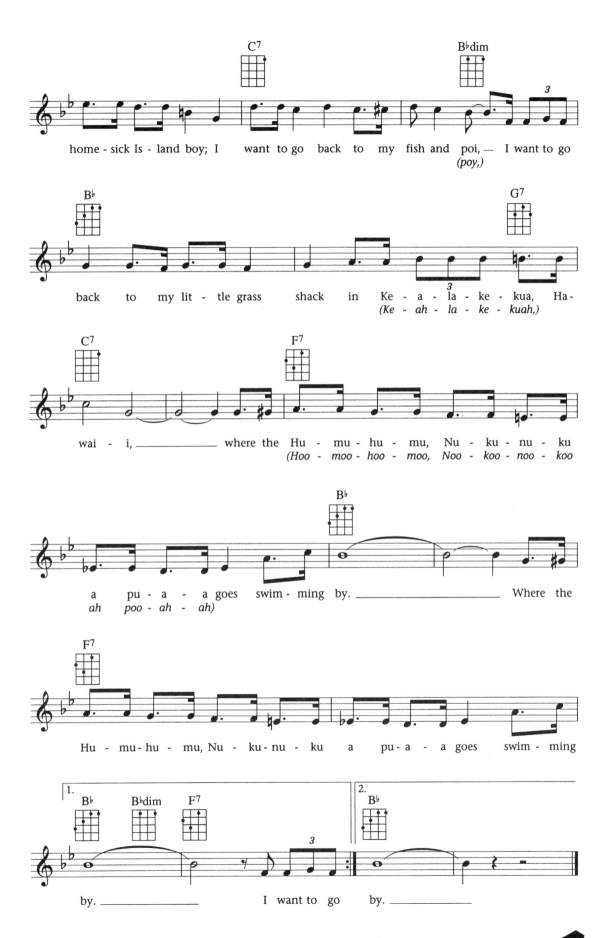

Scratchy Records

Music and Lyrics by
JIM BELOFF

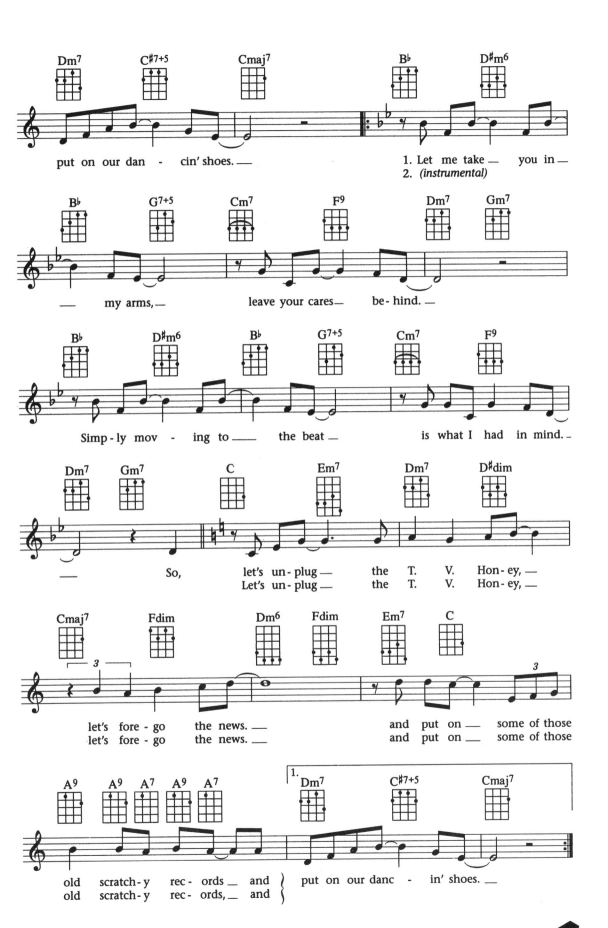

put on our dan - cin' shoes. —

1. Let me take — you in —
2. (instrumental)

— my arms, — leave your cares — be - hind. —

Simp - ly mov - ing to — the beat — is what I had in mind. —

— So, let's un - plug — the T. V. Hon - ey, —
Let's un - plug — the T. V. Hon - ey, —

let's fore - go the news. — and put on — some of those
let's fore - go the news. — and put on — some of those

old scratch - y rec - ords _ and put on our danc - in' shoes. —
old scratch - y rec - ords, _ and

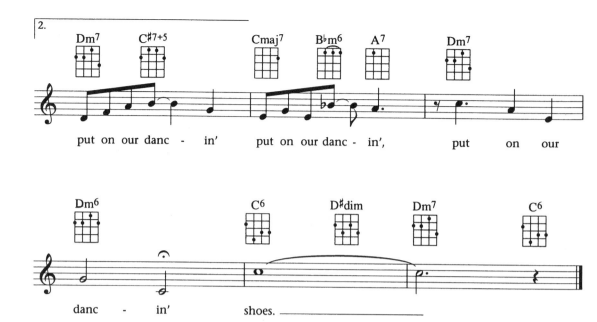

2.

Dm⁷ C♯⁷⁺⁵ Cmaj⁷ B♭m⁶ A⁷ Dm⁷

put on our danc - in' put on our danc - in', put on our

Dm⁶ C⁶ D♯dim Dm⁷ C⁶

danc - in' shoes. —————————

The author at play.

Under Paris Skies
(Sous Le Ciel De Paris)

English Words by
KIM GANNON

French Words by
JEAN DREJAC

Music by
HUBERT GIRAUD

FIRST NOTE

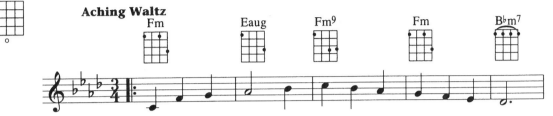

1. Strang-er be-ware, there's love in the air un-der Par-
2. Love be-comes king, the mo-ment it's spring, un-der Par-

is skies. _____ Try to be smart and don't let your
is skies. _____ Lone-ly hearts meet some-where on the

heart catch on fire. _____
street of de-sire. _____

Pa-ri-sian love can bloom, high in a sky-

light room, or in a gay ca-fé where hun-dreds of peo-ple can

see. _____ I was-n't smart and

I lost my heart un-der Par - is skies; _____

don't ev-er be a heart-bro-ken strang-er like me. _____

— Oh, I fell in love. _____ Yes, I was a

fool, _____ for Par-is can be _____

— so beau-ti-f'ly cruel. _____ Par-is is

40

Singin' In The Rain

Words by
ARTHUR FREED

Music by
NACIO HERB BROWN

FIRST NOTE

Chorus, Moderately

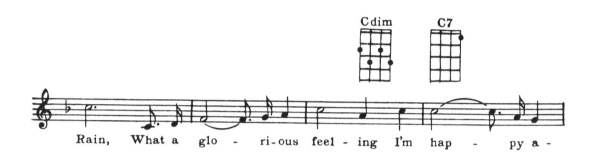

I'm Sing - in' In The Rain, Just Sing - in' In The

Rain, What a glo - ri-ous feel - ing I'm hap - py a -

gain, I'm laugh - ing at clouds so dark up a -

bove, The sun's___ in my heart___ and I'm rea - dy for

love   Let   the   storm - y   clouds   chase   ev-'ry-one ____ from the

C dim   C7

place,   Come   on ____ with   the   rain,   I've   a   smile ____ on my

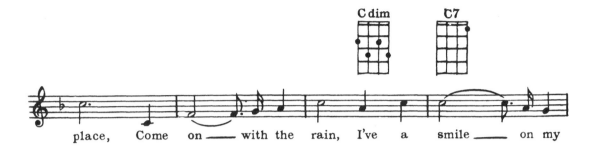

face   I'll   walk   down   the   lane   with   a   hap - py   re -

frain,   And   sing-in' ____   just   Sing-in'   In ____ The

F   F

|1. |2.

Rain. _____   I'm   Rain. _____

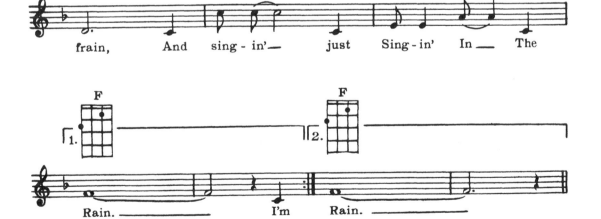

Sonny Boy

By AL JOLSON, B.G. DeSYLVA,
LEW BROWN and RAY HENDERSON

FIRST NOTE

With expression

Climb up - on my knee, son - ny boy;
You're my dear - est prize, son - ny boy;

you are on - ly three, son - ny boy.
sent from out the skies, son - ny boy.

You've no way of know - ing, there's no way of show - ing
Let me hold you near - er, one thing makes you dear - er:

Slowly

what you mean to me, son - ny boy.
you've your moth - er's eyes, son - ny boy.

When there are

gray skies, I don't mind the gray skies;

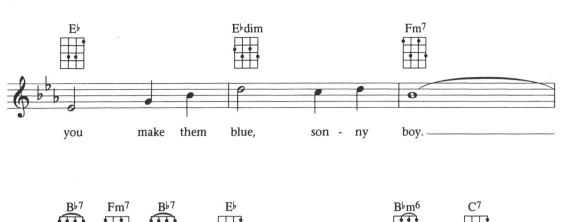

you make them blue, son - ny boy. _____

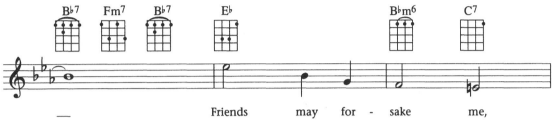

_ Friends may for - sake me,

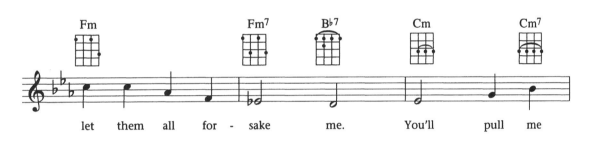

let them all for - sake me. You'll pull me

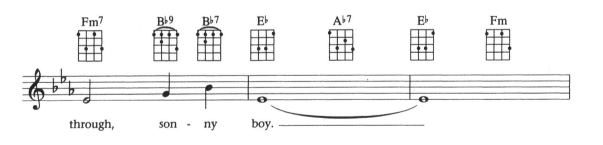

through, son - ny boy. _____

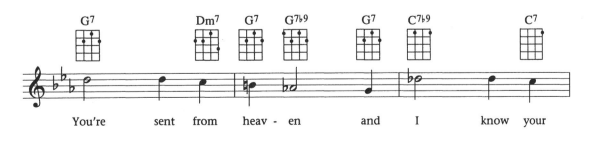

You're sent from heav - en and I know your

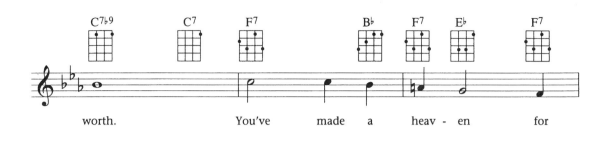

worth. You've made a heav-en for

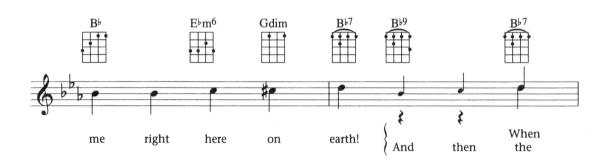

me right here on earth! And then When the

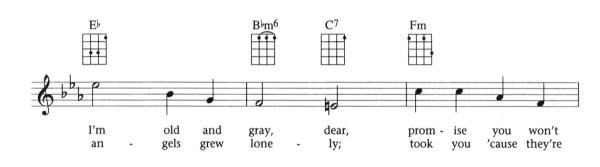

I'm old and gray, dear, prom-ise you won't
an - gels grew lone - ly; took you 'cause they're

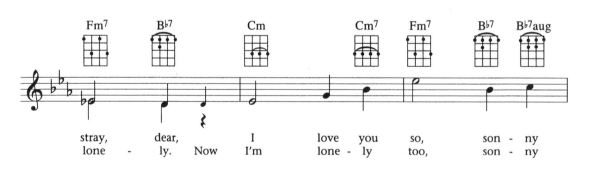

stray, dear, I love you so, son - ny
lone - ly. Now I'm lone - ly too, son - ny

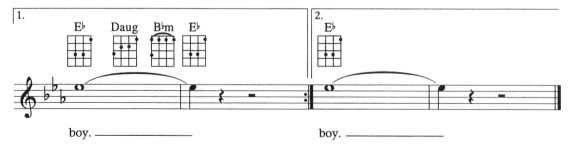

boy. _____ boy. _____

46

Sunny Side Up

By
B.G. De SYLVA, LEW BROWN
and RAY HENDERSON

47

Ukulele Lady

Lyric by
GUS KAHN

Music by
RICHARD A. WHITING

First Note

Moderato

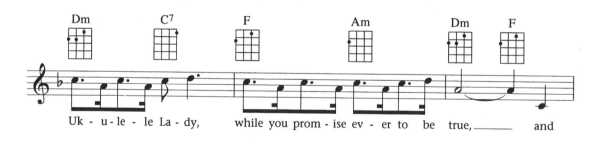

If you like - a Uk - u - le - le La - dy,

Uk - u - le - le La - dy like - a you. _____ If you like to

lin - ger where it's sha - dy, Uk - u - le - le La - dy lin - ger too. If you kiss a

Uk - u - le - le La - dy, while you prom - ise ev - er to be true, _____ and

she see an - oth - er Uk - u - le - le La - dy fool a - round with

48

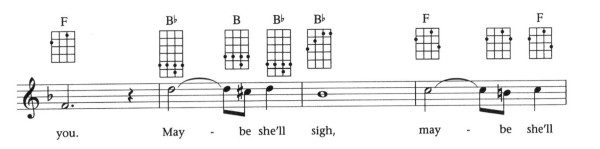

you. May - be she'll sigh, may - be she'll

cry, may - be she'll find some-bod - y else by and

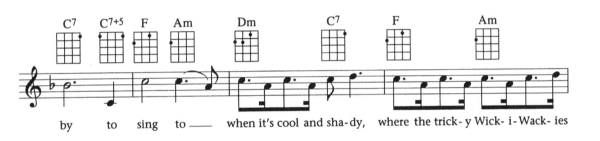

by to sing to —— when it's cool and sha-dy, where the trick- y Wick- i- Wack- ies

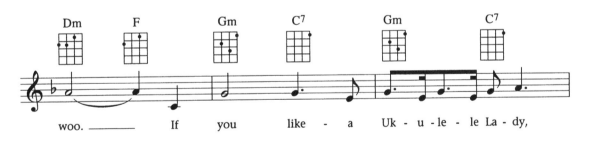

woo. ———— If you like - a Uk - u -le - le La -dy,

Uk - u -le - le La -dy like - a you. If you.

When The Red, Red, Robin
Comes Bob, Bob, Bobbin' Along

Lyrics and Music by
HARRY WOODS

laugh and be hap - py. What if I've been blue, now I'm walk - in' through

fields of flow'rs. Rain may glis - ten, but

still I lis - ten for hours and hours.

I'm just a kid a - gain, do - in' what I did a - gain, sing - ing a

song, when the red, red, rob - in comes bob, bob, bob - bin' a -

1. long. When the **2.** long. _____

Yes Sir, That's My Baby

Lyric by
GUS KAHN

Music by
WALTER DONALDSON

FIRST NOTE

Yes, sir, that's my ba - by, no, sir,

don't mean "may - be" Yes, sir, that's my ba - by

now. _____

Yes, ma'am we've de - cid - ed,
Well, well, "lookit" that ba - by,

no, ma'am, we won't hide it. Yes, ma'am, you're in - vit - ed
do tell, don't say, "may-be." Nell's bells, won't she cause some

You're The Cream In My Coffee

By B.G. DeSYLVA
LEW BROWN and
RAY HENDERSON

Bye Bye Blues

Words & Music by
FRED HAMM, DAVE BENNETT,
BERT LOWN and CHAUNCEY GRAY

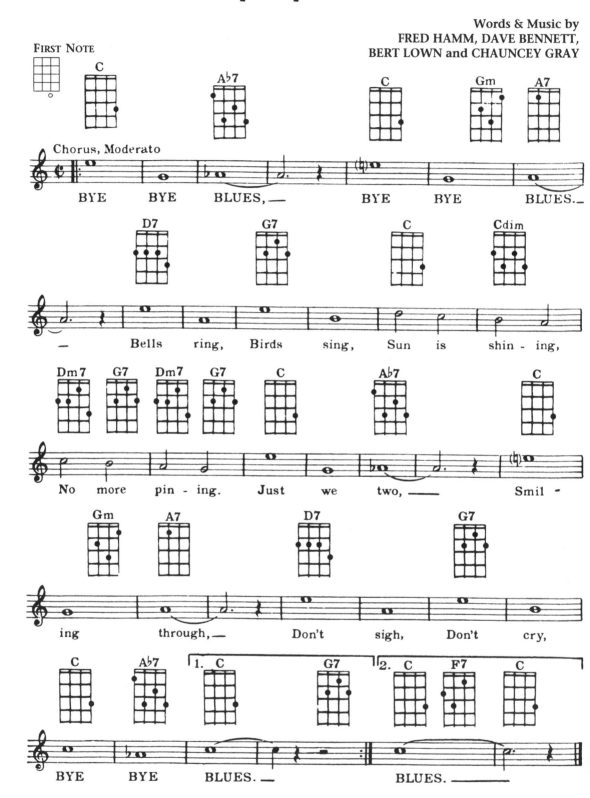

Ukulele Chord Solos

The following six songs are arranged as chord solos. This is accomplished by combining both the melody and the harmony in the arrangement. Because there is chordal movement for virtually every note in the melody, these arrangements require a good deal of practice and patience. The good news is that, once mastered, these types of arrangements can be some of the most satisfying pieces you can play for yourself and others. They really become show pieces.

To get your fingers "wet," you may want to start with "Ain't She Sweet." This is a fairly simple arrangement. Also, note that the fingerings below the chords are suggestions. If you can find a smoother way to move from chord to chord, and still have the melody prominent, go for it. Pay attention, though, to the instances of "pick" notes (the first two chord frames in "Seems Like Old Times," for example), where you are instructed to pick only a single note:

Example 1

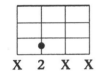

Pick only the 3rd string
at the third fret.

Example 2

Pick only the 3rd string
at the fourth fret.

Finally, figuring out good arrangements can be even more fun than playing them. I invite you to try your hand(s) at coming up with chord solos for your own favorite songs.

Gus Kahn, lyricist for "I'll See You In My Dreams," "It Had To Be You,"
"Ukulele Lady," and "Yes Sir! That's My Baby."
(Photo courtesy of Donald Kahn)

Ain't She Sweet

Words by
JACK YELLEN

Music by
MILTON AGER

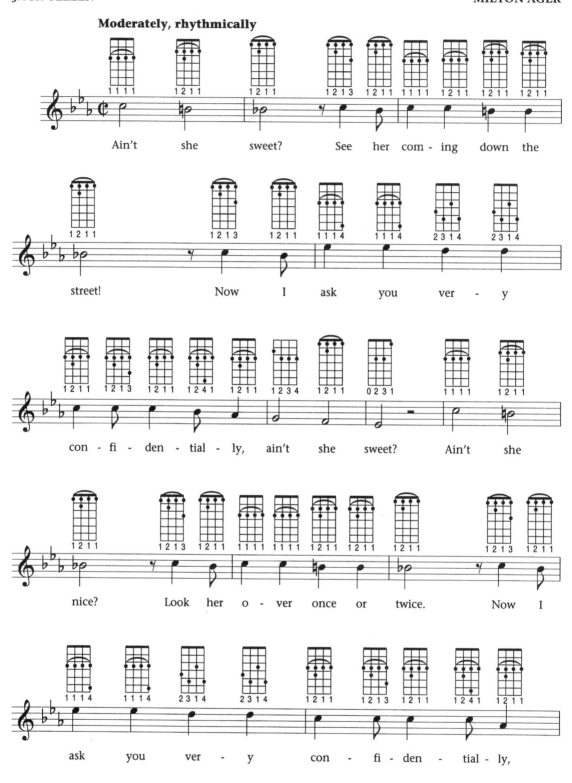

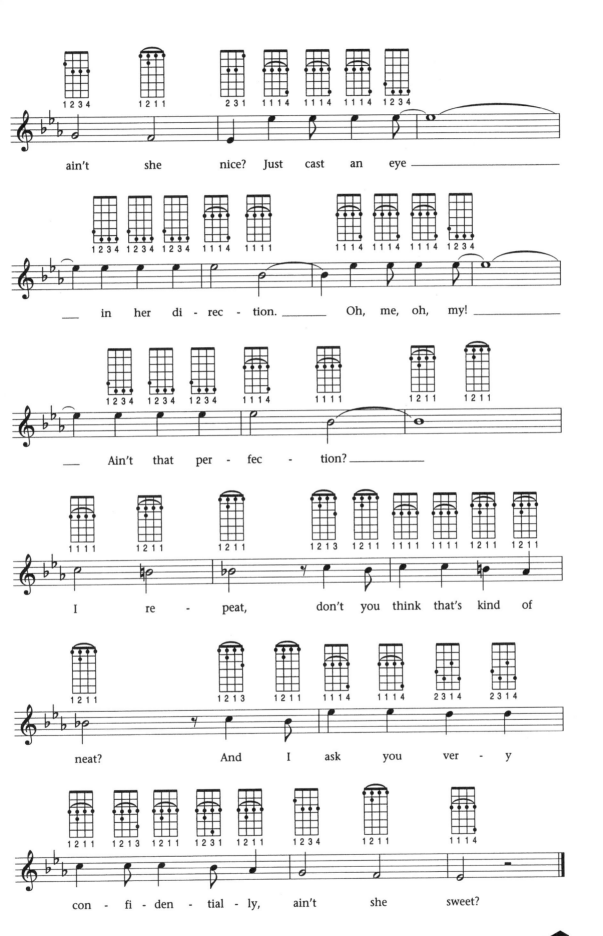

ain't she nice? Just cast an eye _____

___ in her di - rec - tion. ___ Oh, me, oh, my! ___

___ Ain't that per - fec - tion? _____

I re - peat, don't you think that's kind of

neat? And I ask you ver - y

con - fi - den - tial - ly, ain't she sweet?

All Of Me

Music and Words by
SEYMOUR SIMONS
and GERALD MARKS

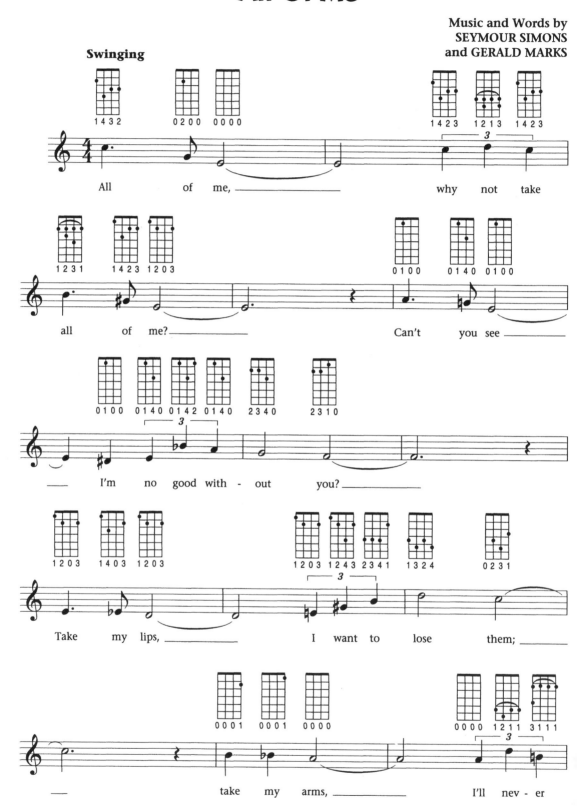

Swinging

All of me, _____ why not take

all of me? _____ Can't you see _____

_____ I'm no good with - out you? _____

Take my lips, _____ I want to lose them; _____

_____ take my arms, _____ I'll nev - er

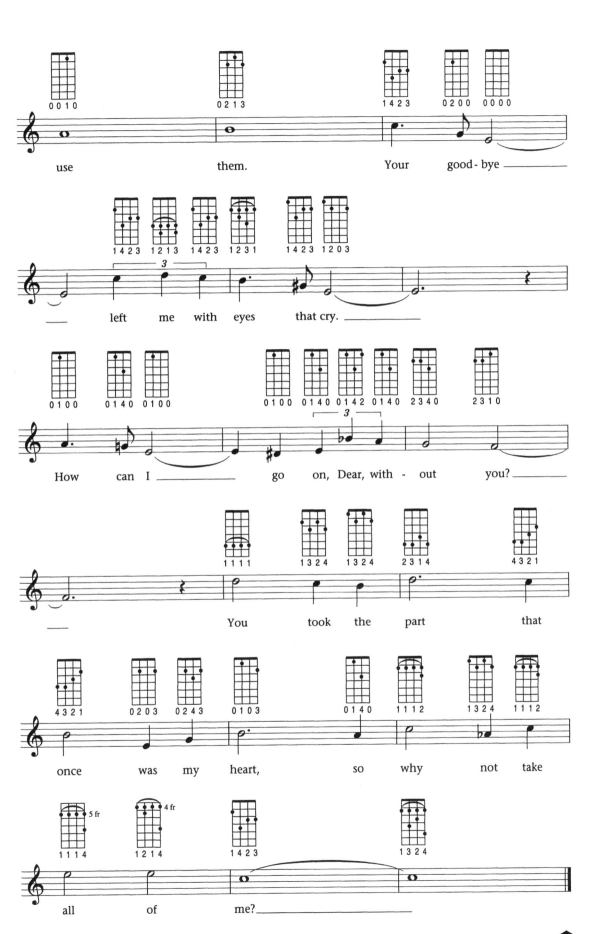

Seems Like Old Times

Words and Music by
JOHN JACOB LOEB
and CARMEN LOMBARDO

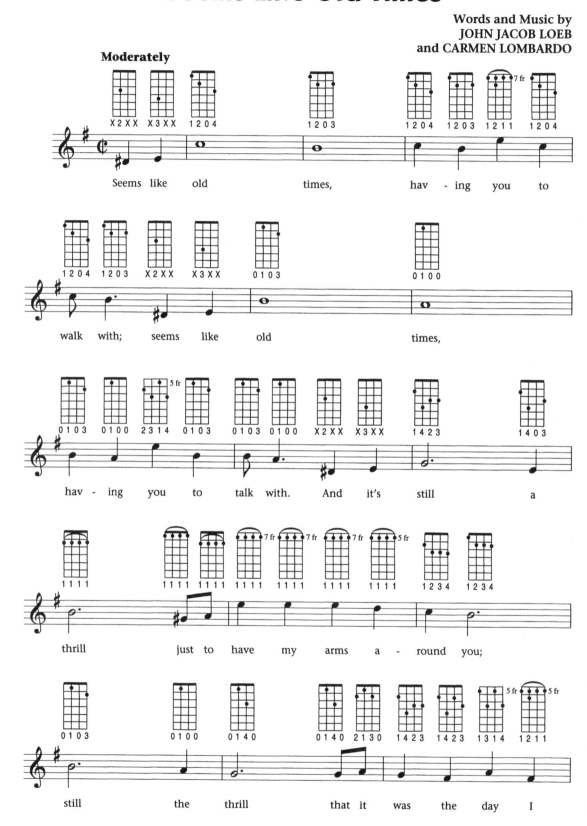

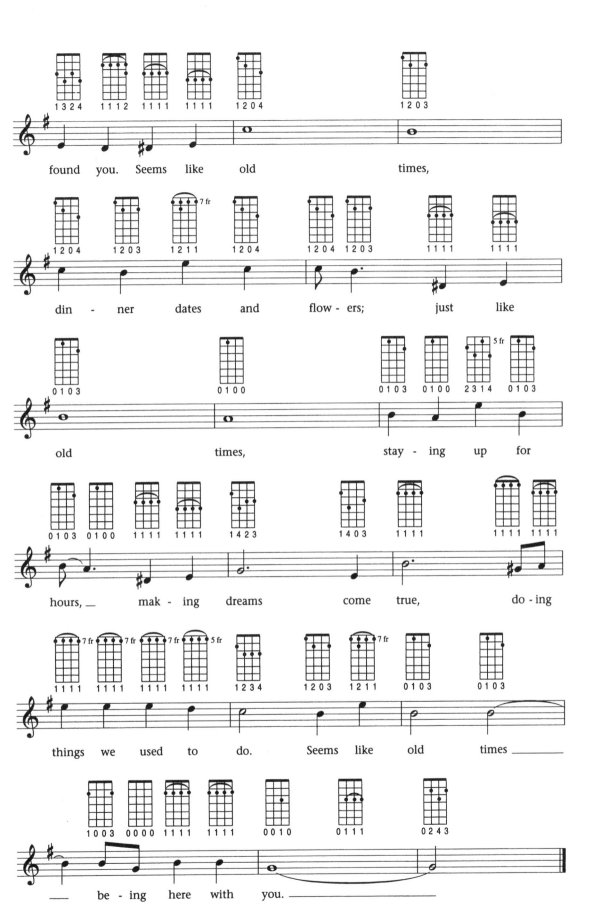

Sentimental Journey

By BUD GREEN,
LES BROWN and BEN HOMER

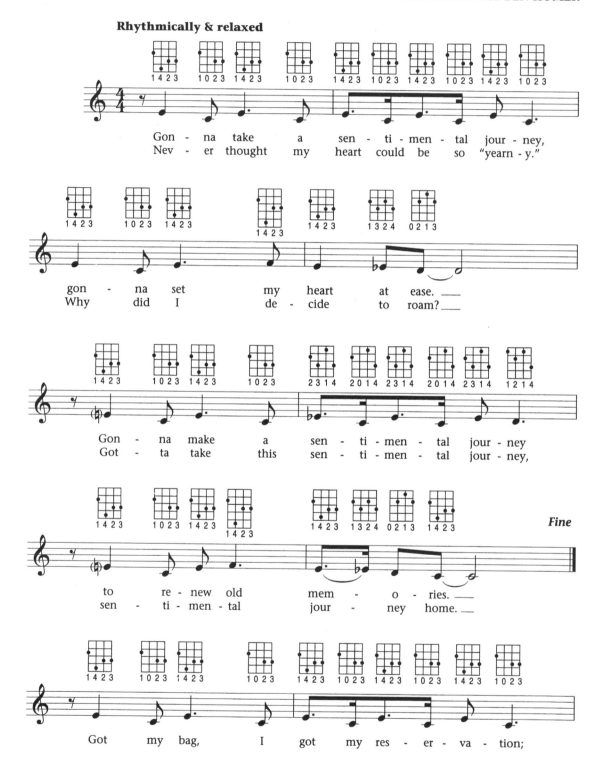

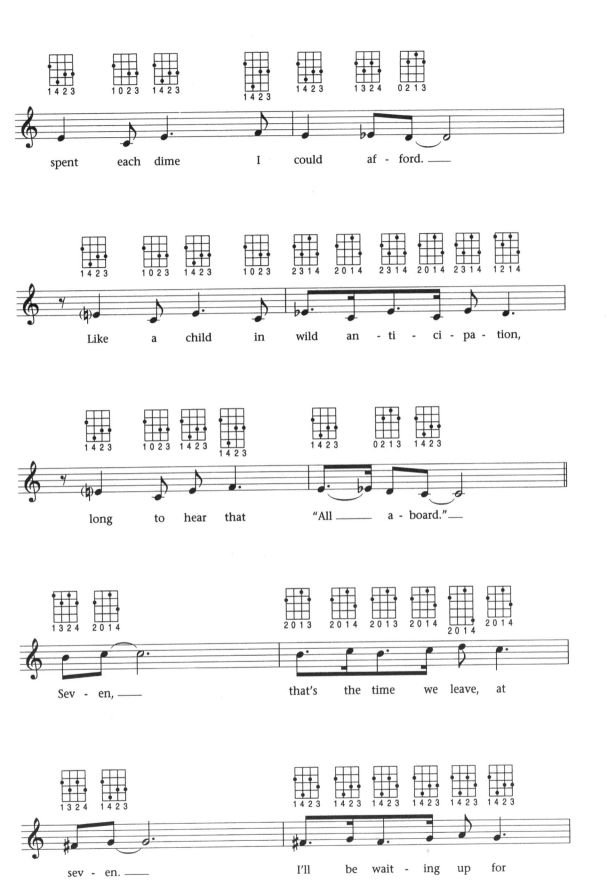

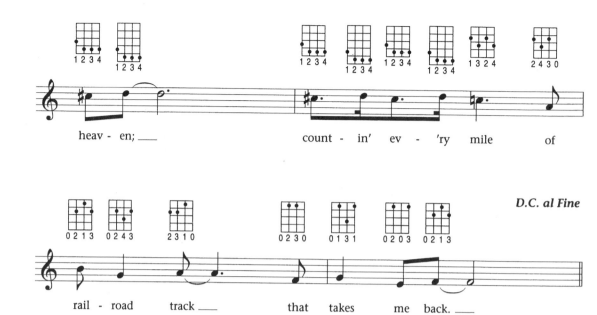

heav - en; _____ count - in' ev - 'ry mile of

D.C. al Fine

rail - road track _____ that takes me back. _____

...Every one a "gem"—and arranged for ukulele, of course!

'Til There Was You

By
MEREDITH WILLSON

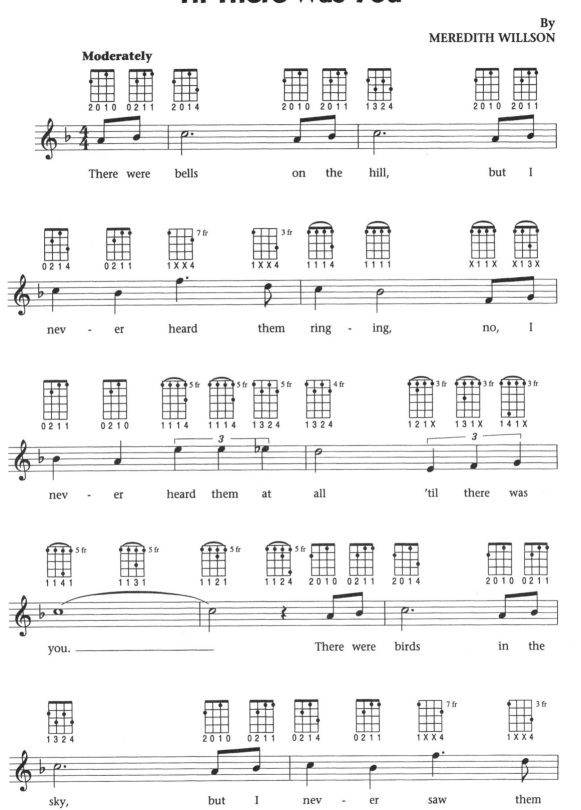

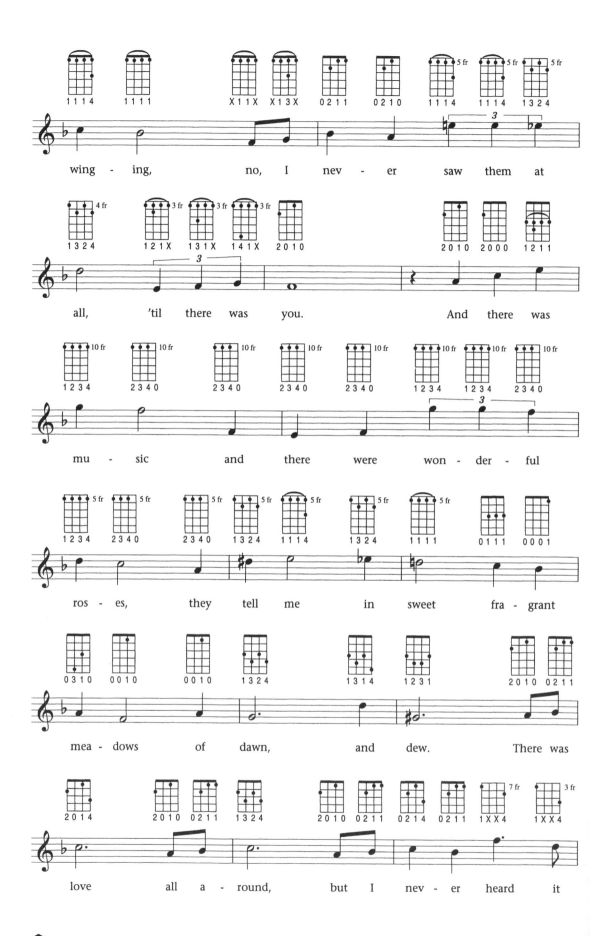

wing - ing, no, I nev - er saw them at all, 'til there was you. And there was mu - sic and there were won - der - ful ros - es, they tell me in sweet fra - grant mea - dows of dawn, and dew. There was love all a - round, but I nev - er heard it

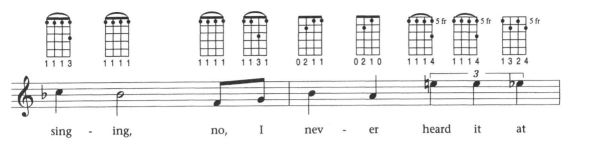

sing - ing,   no,   I   nev - er   heard   it   at

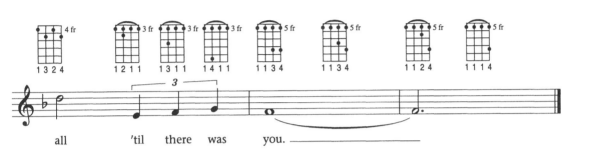

all   'til   there   was   you. ———————

Flea market sheet music; Sonny and Sunny in the sun.

When You Wish Upon A Star

Lyric by
NED WASHINGTON

Music by
LEIGH HARLINE

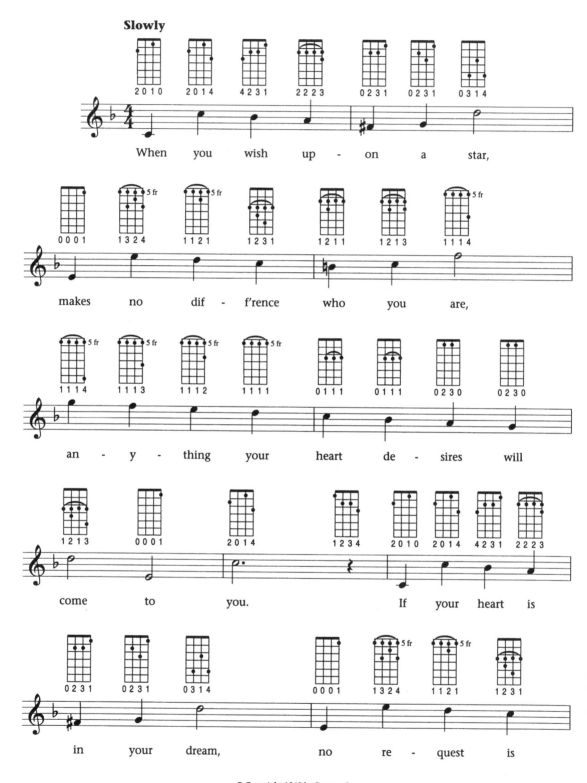

When you wish up - on a star, makes no dif - f'rence who you are, an - y - thing your heart de - sires will come to you. If your heart is in your dream, no re - quest is

too ex - treme, when you wish u -

pon a star as dream - ers do.

Fate is kind, she brings to

those who love the sweet ful -

fill - ment of their se - cret long -

ing. Like a bolt out of the blue,

71

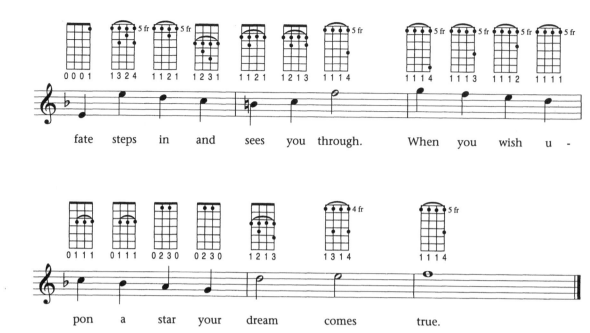

fate   steps   in   and   sees   you   through.   When   you   wish   u -

pon   a   star   your   dream   comes   true.

Walter Donaldson, music for "Yes Sir! That's My Baby."
(Photo courtesy of Ellen Donaldson)